ACE THE PENNSYLVANIA NOTARY PUBLIC EXAM QUESTIONS AND ANSWERS

225 Questions and Answers in Flash-Card Format

Angelo Tropea

ISBN 13: 978-1721851706

ISBN 10: 1721851704

Please note that laws and regulations relating
to notaries public are available for free in
many places, including online at:
http://www.dos.pa.gov/OtherServices/Notaries/Resources/
Pages/Laws-.aspx

CONTENTS

"Notaries Public…hold an office which can trace its origins back to ancient Rome when they were called *scribae, tabellius* or *notarius*. They are easily the oldest continuing branch of the legal profession worldwide."*

THE AIM OF THIS BOOK

The Pennsylvania Department of State, "Notaries" webpage provides important information, such as:

1. Becoming a Notary/Notary Services

2. General Information and Equipment

3. Notary Education Course Approval

4. Resources

-and other links to help you pass the Notary Public Exam and be a well-informed notary public.

The aim of this book is to complement the official information and classes by providing questions and answers to help you better prepare for the exam and become a more knowledgeable and professional practicing notary public.

THIS BOOK PROVIDES:

1. True/False, fill-in and other "Quick Questions" to help you remember facts and definitions.

2. Multiple choice questions to help you practice for the notary public exam.

All the 225 questions are in flash card format – a popular and effective method of preparing for exams.

We believe that the combination of the above will provide the tools and the required practice to help you achieve your goal of passing the notary public exam and also increase your understanding and appreciation of laws important to notaries public.

For detailed information on how to apply for the Notary Public Exam, please visit:

http://www.dos.pa.gov/OtherServices/Notaries/Pages/default.aspx#.VSZ6KvDD-KU

HOW TO USE THIS BOOK

There are probably as many ways to study successfully as there are people. However, in the more than twenty-five years preparing study materials and conducting classes for civil service exams, I have found that certain methods seem to work better than others with the great majority of students. The following are time tested suggestions that you might want to consider as you incorporate this book in the study plan that is best for you.

SUGGESTIONS:

1. Try the "Quick Questions" first. Do not go on to the multiple-choice questions until you have mastered these questions. Read the comments after each answer to reinforce important facts.

2. After the "Quick Questions" practice with the multiple-choice questions. On the actual test you will have around 30 multiple-choice questions.

Study every day. Take this book with you – and make it your friend.

The actual laws and regulations are available in many places, including for free online at:

http://www.dos.pa.gov/OtherServices/Notaries/Resources/Pages/Laws-.aspx

NOTARY PUBLIC LAWS AND REGULATIONS

The following is a list of laws and regulations relating to notaries public. The flash cards in this book are drawn from these statutes.

LAW
The Notary Public Law (Jul. 1, 2003)

Section	Description
1	Short Title
2	Appointment of Notaries
3	Eligibility
4	Disqualification; Exception
5	Application to Become a Notary Public
6	Application for Reappointment
7	Vacation of Office
8	Oath of Office; Bond; Recording
9	Registration of Notary's Signature; Fee
10	Change of Name
11	Refund of Fee (Repealed June 30, 1888)
12	Notarial Seal
13	Date of Expiration of Commission (Repealed 6/30/1988)

14	Position of Seal and Date of Expiration of Commission (Repealed June 30, 1988)
15	Register; Copies of Records
16	Power to Administer Oaths and Affirmations
17	Power to take Acknowledgment of Instruments of Writing Relating to Commerce or Navigation and to Make Declarations (Repealed by 2002)
18	Power to Take Depositions, Affidavits and Acknowledgment of Writings Relative to Lands (Repealed 2002, Dec. 9)
19	Limitations on Powers; Fees
20	Admissibility in Evidence (Repealed April 28, 1978)
21	Fees of Notaries Public
22	Rejection of Application; Removal
22.1	Surrender of Seal
22.2	Revocation of Commission for Certain Personal Checks
22.3	Regulations
23	Specific Repeal
24	Repeals

Pennsylvania's Revised Uniform Law on Notarial Acts (RULONA: effective October 26, 2017)

Section	Description and Page Number
301	Short title of chapter
302	Definitions
303	Applicability
304	Authority to perform notarial act
305	Requirements for certain notarial acts
306	Personal appearance required
307	Identification of individual
308	Authority to refuse to perform notarial act
309	Signature if individual unable to sign (Reserved)
310	Notarial act in this Commonwealth
311	Notarial act in another state
312	Notarial act under authority of federally recognized Indian tribe
313	Notarial act under federal authority
314	Foreign notarial act
315	Certificate of notarial act
316	Short form certificates

317	Official stamp
318	Stamping device
319	Journal
320	Notification regarding performance of notarial act on electronic record; selection of technology
321	Appointment and commission as notary public; qualifications; no immunity or benefit
322	Examination, basic education and continuing education
323	Sanctions
324	Database of notaries public
325	Prohibited acts
326	Validity of notarial acts
327	Regulations
328	Notary public commission in effect
329	Savings clause
329.1	Fees of notaries public
330	Uniformity of application and construction
331	Relation to electronic Signatures in Global and National Commerce Act

NOTARIES PUBLIC (57 PA.C.S.) - OMNIBUS AMENDMENTS
Act of Jul. 9, 2014, P.L. 1035, No. 119   Cl. 57
Session of 2014

1 - 7.1	Omnibus Amendments

UNIFORM ACKNOWLEDGMENT ACT(*)

(Act No. 188, approved July 24, 1941, as amended by Acts 353 and 354 of 1947, Act 3 of 1951, Act 58 of 1957, Act 61 of 1961 and Act 71 of 1981)

1 - 14	Types of Acknowledgments, Certificate Forms

RULONA REGULATIONS - Proposed August 2016
Selected Sections

161.1 - 167.127	Selected sections

QUESTION AND ANSWER FORMAT

Questions are individual cards.

The answer to each question is on the following page.

In addition to the answer, there is more information.

For deeper understanding and retention, study both the

answer and the additional information.

REMINDER

The flash cards in this book are not a replacement

for reading the law. They are a study tool.

After a careful review of the law, use the study cards

(flash cards) to help you reinforce your understanding and

memory of the law.

STUDY DEEP

This will not only help you pass the exam,

but it will also help you become a more knowledgeable,

respected, and professional notary public!

———————

SUGGESTIONS:

QUICK QUESTIONS
(Pages 13 - 70)

1. Try the "Quick Questions" (True/False and Fill-ins) first.
   - Read the comments after each answer to reinforce important facts.
   - If you answer incorrectly, read that section of law or regulations to reinforce your memory.
   - Do not go on to the multiple-choice questions until you have mastered these questions.

MULTIPLE-CHOICE QUESTIONS
(Pages 71- 124)

2. After the "Quick Questions" practice with the Multiple-Choice Questions.
   - On the actual test you will have around 30 multiple-choice questions.
   - Do not write your answer in the book. Use a separate piece of paper. This way you can retake the test without being influenced by your prior answers.

Study every day.

Take this book with you – and make it your friend!

QUICK QUESTIONS

Notary Public Law: Section 2
The Secretary of the Commonwealth is authorized to appoint and commission notaries public for a term of _____ years from the date of appointment.

Notary Public Law: Section 2
The jurisdiction of notaries public is coextensive with the boundaries of the _____.

Notary Public Law: Section 3
Any person who is ___ years of age or over, who resides or is employed within this Commonwealth and who is of good character, integrity and ability shall be eligible for the office of notary public.

Notary Public Law: Section 3
Any person who is a notary public and who resides outside this Commonwealth shall be deemed to have irrevocably appointed the _____ as the person's agent upon whom may be served any summons, subpoena, order or other process.

Notary Public Law: Section 5
Applications for appointment to the office of notary public shall be made to the _____.

ANSWERS

four

The Secretary of the Commonwealth is authorized to appoint and commission notaries public for a term of **four** years from the date of appointment.

Commonwealth

The jurisdiction of notaries public is coextensive with the boundaries of the **Commonwealth**.

18
Any person who is eighteen **(18)** years of age or over, who resides or is employed within this Commonwealth and who is of good character, integrity and ability shall be eligible for the office of notary public.

Notary Public Law: Section 3
Any person who is a notary public and who resides outside this Commonwealth shall be deemed to have irrevocably appointed the **Secretary of the Commonwealth** as the person's agent upon whom may be served any summons, subpoena, order or other process.

Secretary of the Commonwealth

Applications for appointment to the office of notary public shall be made to the **Secretary of the Commonwealth.**

QUICK QUESTIONS

Notary Public Law: Section 5
An applicant for notary public shall not have been convicted of or pled guilty or "nolo contendere" to a felony or a lesser offense incompatible with the duties of a notary public during the _____ year period preceding the date of the application.

Notary Public Law: Section 5
A notary applicant must complete at least ___ hours of approved notary education within the ___ month period immediately preceding his application.

Notary Public Law: Section 6
Application for Reappointment. Applications for reappointment to the office of notary public shall be filed at least ___ months prior to the expiration of the commission under which the notary is acting.

Notary Public Law: Section 7
If the notary changes his office address within the Commonwealth, notice in writing or electronically shall be given to the Secretary and the recorder of deeds of the county of original appointment by the notary within ___ days of such change.

Notary Public Law: Section 7
A notary public vacates his office by removing the notary's residence and _____ address from the Commonwealth, and such removal shall constitute a resignation from the office of notary public as of the date of removal.

ANSWERS

5

An applicant for notary public shall not have been convicted of or pled guilty or "nolo contendere" to a felony or a lesser offense incompatible with the duties of a notary public during the **5**-year period preceding the date of the application.

3....6

A notary applicant must complete at least three **3** hours of approved notary education within the **6**-month period immediately preceding his application.

2

Application for Reappointment. Applications for reappointment to the office of notary public shall be filed at least **2** months prior to the expiration of the commission under which the notary is acting.

5

If the notary changes his office address within the Commonwealth, notice in writing or electronically shall be given to the Secretary and the recorder of deeds of the county of original appointment by the notary within **5** days of such change.

business

A notary public vacates his office by removing the notary's residence and **business** address from the Commonwealth, and such removal shall constitute a resignation from the office of notary public as of the date of removal.

QUICK QUESTIONS

Notary Public Law: Section 8
Every notary, upon appointment and prior to entering the duties of notary public, shall take and subscribe the constitutional oath of office, and shall give a surety bond, payable to the Commonwealth of Pennsylvania, in the amount of $_____.

Notary Public Law: Section 8
Every notary bond shall have as surety a duly authorized surety company or _____ sufficient individual sureties, to be approved by the Secretary of the Commonwealth, conditioned for the faithful performance of the duties of the office of notary public.

Notary Public Law: Section 8
The notary bond ensures the faithful performance of the notary's duties and the delivery of notary's register and seal to the office of the recorder of deeds of the proper county in case of the death, resignation or disqualification of the notary within _____ days of such event.

Notary Public Law: Section 8
The notary public bond, as well as the commission and oath of office, shall be recorded in the _____ of the county in which the notary maintains an office at the time of appointment or reappointment.

Notary Public Law: Section 8
If a notary public fails to give bond and cause the bond and the commission and oath to be recorded within ___ days after the beginning of the term, his commission shall be null and void.

ANSWERS

$10,000

Every notary, upon appointment and prior to entering the duties of notary public, shall take and subscribe the constitutional oath of office, and shall give a surety bond, payable to the Commonwealth of Pennsylvania, in the amount of **ten thousand dollars ($ 10,000)**.

two

Every notary bond shall have as surety a duly authorized surety company or **two** sufficient individual sureties, to be approved by the Secretary of the Commonwealth, conditioned for the faithful performance of the duties of the office of notary public.

30

The notary bond ensures the faithful performance of the notary's duties and the delivery of notary's register and seal to the office of the recorder of deeds of the proper county in case of the death, resignation or disqualification of the notary within thirty **(30)** days of such event.

office of the recorder of deeds

The notary public bond, as well as the commission and oath of office, shall be recorded in the **office of the recorder of deeds** of the county in which the notary maintains an office at the time of appointment or reappointment.

45

If a notary public fails to give bond and cause the bond and the commission and oath to be recorded within **(45)** days after the beginning of the term, his commission shall be null and void.

QUICK QUESTIONS

Notary Public Law: Section 9
The official notary signature shall be registered, in the "Notary Register" in the prothonotary's office of county where the notary maintains an office, within _____ days after appointment or reappointment.

Notary Public Law: Section 9
If a notary moves his office to another county, he must within _____ days thereafter register his signature in the prothonotary's office of county where the notary maintains an office.

Notary Public Law: Section 9
In acting as a notary public, a notary shall sign the notary's name exactly and only as it appears on the _____ or otherwise execute the notary's electronic signature in a manner that attributes such signature to the notary public identified on the commission.

Notary Public Law: Section 10
Change of Name. Whenever the name of any notary is changed by decree of court, or otherwise, such notary may continue to perform official acts, in the name in which he was commissioned, until the _____.

Notary Public Law: Section 10
When a notary changes his name, he must within thirty (30) days after entry of a name change decree, or after such name change, if not by decree of court, notify the _____ of such name change.

ANSWERS

45

The official notary signature shall be registered, in the "Notary Register" in the prothonotary's office of county where the notary maintains an office, within **45** days after appointment or reappointment. (In counties of the second class, such signature shall also be registered in the clerk of courts' office within said period.)

30

If a notary moves his office to another county, he must within **30** days thereafter register his signature in the prothonotary's office of county where the notary maintains an office. (In counties of the second class, such signature shall also be registered in the clerk of courts' office within said period.)

commission

In acting as a notary public, a notary shall sign the notary's name exactly and only as it appears on the **commission** or otherwise execute the notary's electronic signature in a manner that attributes such signature to the notary public identified on the commission.

expiration of his term

Change of Name. Whenever the name of any notary is changed by decree of court, or otherwise, such notary may continue to perform official acts, in the name in which he was commissioned, until the **expiration of his term.**

Secretary of the Commonwealth and recorder of deeds of county where he maintains an office

When a notary changes his name, he must within thirty (30) days after entry of a name change decree, or after such name change, if not by decree of court, notify the **Secretary of the Commonwealth and recorder of deeds of county where he maintains an office** of such name change.

QUICK QUESTIONS

Notary Public Law: Section 12
When certifying a copy of a document or other item, what must a notary public do?

Notary Public Law: Section 22.1
If an application or renewal is rejected, or a commission is revoked or recalled, or if a notary public resigns, applicant or notary shall deliver the seal to the Department of State within _____ days after notice from the department or from date of resignation, as the case may be.

Notary Public Law: Section 22.1 (Surrender of Seal)
Any person who violates the provisions of this subsection shall be guilty of a summary offense and upon conviction thereof shall be sentenced to pay a fine not exceeding $_____ or to imprisonment not exceeding _____ days, or both.

RULONA 304

A notarial officer (may / may not) perform a notarial act with respect to a record in which the notarial officer or the notarial officer's spouse has a direct or pecuniary interest.

RULONA 305
Notarial officer who takes an acknowledgment of a record shall determine, from _____ or satisfactory evidence of the identity of the person, that the Person appearing before notarial officer and making the acknowledgment is the person claimed.

ANSWERS

When certifying a copy of a document or other item, a notary public <u>shall determine that the proffered copy is a full, true and accurate transcription or reproduction of that which was copied</u>.

If an application or renewal is rejected, or a commission is revoked or recalled, or if a notary public resigns, applicant or notary shall deliver the seal to the Department of State within **ten (10)** days after notice from the department or from date of resignation, as the case may be.

Any person who violates the provisions of this subsection shall be guilty of a summary offense and upon conviction thereof shall be sentenced to pay a fine not exceeding **three hundred dollars ($ 300)** or to imprisonment not exceeding **ninety (90) days**, or both.

may not

A notarial officer **may not** perform a notarial act with respect to a record in which the notarial officer or the notarial officer's spouse has a direct or pecuniary interest.

Notarial officer who takes an acknowledgment of a record shall determine, from **personal knowledge** or satisfactory evidence of the identity of the person, that the Person appearing before notarial officer and making the acknowledgment is the person claimed.

QUICK QUESTIONS

RULONA 301

RULONA is the abbreviation for _____.

RULONA 302

"_____" is a declaration made in front of a notary that:
   (1) the person signed the record for the reason stated in the record; and that
   (2) if the person signed as a representative, he did so with proper authority.

RULONA 302

T/F? The definition for "Conviction" does not have to include a sentence ordered by the court.

RULONA 302

An electronic symbol, sound or process attached to or logically associated with a record and executed or adopted by an individual with the intent to sign the record is known as _____.

RULONA 302

T/F? A signature does not have to be in written form.

ANSWERS

RULONA is the abbreviation for
"Revised Uniform Law on Notarial Acts"

"Acknowledgment" is a declaration made in front of a notary that:
   (1) the person signed the record for the reason stated in the record; and that
   (2) if the person signed as a representative, he did so with proper authority.

True
"Conviction" means any of the following, even if a sentence was <u>not</u> ordered by a court:
   (1) An entry of a plea of guilty or "no contest".
   (2) A guilty verdict in a trial (with or without a jury).
   (3) Not guilty due to insanity, or guilty but mentally ill.

electronic signature

An electronic symbol, sound or process attached to or logically associated with a record and executed or adopted by an individual with the intent to sign the record is known as an **electronic signature**.

True

"Signature." can be a tangible symbol <u>or an electronic signature</u> which evidences the signing of a record.

QUICK QUESTIONS

RULONA 302

T/F? A stamping device can be physical or electronic.

RULONA 302

"_____" is a declaration made by an individual on oath or affirmation before a notarial officer, that a statement in a record is true. The term includes an affidavit.

RULONA 304
A notarial officer (may/may not) perform a notarial act with respect to a record in which the notarial officer or notarial officer's spouse has a direct or pecuniary interest.

RULONA 304
If a notary public performs a notarial act in which he has a pecuniary interest in the transaction, the notarial act is

_____.

RULONA 305
A notarial officer who takes a verification of a statement on oath or affirmation shall determine identity from personal knowledge or _____ of the identity of the person.

ANSWERS

True
"Stamping device." Any of the following:
- (1) A physical device capable of affixing to or embossing on a tangible record an official stamp.
- (2) An electronic device or process capable of attaching to or logically associating with an electronic record an official stamp.

"Verification on oath or affirmation"
"**Verification on oath or affirmation**" is a declaration, made by an individual on oath or affirmation before a notarial officer, that a statement in a record is true. The term includes an affidavit.

may not

A notarial officer **may not** perform a notarial act with respect to a record in which the notarial officer or notarial officer's spouse has a direct or pecuniary interest.

voidable

If a notary public performs a notarial act in which he has a pecuniary interest in the transaction, the notarial act is **voidable**.

satisfactory evidence
A notarial officer who takes a verification of a statement on oath or affirmation shall determine identity from personal knowledge or **satisfactory evidence** of the identity of the person.

QUICK QUESTIONS

RULONA 306
If a notarial act relates to a statement made in or a signature executed on a record, person making statement or executing signature shall appear _____ before the notary.

RULONA 307
T/F? Satisfactory evidence of identity includes verification on oath or affirmation of a credible witness personally appearing before the notarial officer.

RULONA 308
Before a notary performs a notarial act, the notary must be satisfied that the individual executing the record is competent or has the capacity to execute the record.

RULONA 310
The signature and title of a notarial officer (does / does not) establish the authority of the notarial officer to perform the notarial act.

RULONA 310
Signature and title of an individual performing a notarial act in this Commonwealth are prima facie evidence that: (1) signature is genuine; and (2) _____.

ANSWERS

personally

If a notarial act relates to a statement made in or a signature executed on a record, person making statement or executing signature shall appear **personally** before the notary.

False

Satisfactory evidence of identity includes verification on oath or affirmation of a credible witness personally appearing before the notarial officer **and personally known to the notarial officer**.

True

The notary must also be satisfied that the individual's signature is knowingly and voluntarily made.

does

The signature and title of a notarial officer **does** establish the authority of the notarial officer to perform the notarial act.

individual holds designated title.

Signature and title of an individual performing a notarial act in this Commonwealth are prima facie evidence that: (1) signature is genuine; and (2) **individual holds designated title.**

QUICK QUESTIONS

RULONA 311
Does a notarial act performed in another state have the same effect under the law of this Commonwealth?

RULONA 312
Does a notarial act performed under the authority of a federally recognized Indian tribe have the same effect under the law of this Commonwealth?

RULONA 313
Does a notarial act performed under Federal authority have the same effect under the law of this Commonwealth?

RULONA 314
Does a notarial act performed under the authority of a foreign state have the same effect under the law of this Commonwealth?

RULONA 315
A notarial act shall be evidenced by a _____.

ANSWERS

Yes. Generally, it has the same effect
A notarial act performed in another state has the same effect under the law of this Commonwealth as if performed by a notarial officer of this Commonwealth if the act performed in that state is performed by a notary of that state, judge, clerk or other authorized individual.

Yes. Generally, it has the same effect
A notarial act performed under the authority of a federally recognized Indian tribe has the same effect under the law of this Commonwealth as if performed by a notarial officer of this Commonwealth if the act was performed by a notary, judge, clerk or other authorized individual of tribe.

Yes. Generally, it has the same effect
A notarial act performed under Federal authority has the same effect under the law of this Commonwealth as if performed by a notarial officer of this Commonwealth if the act was performed by a notary, judge, clerk or other Federally authorized individual.

Yes.
Also, a notarial act performed under the authority of a multinational or international governmental organization has the same effect under the law of this Commonwealth. This applies also to the Hague Convention and Consular authentications.

certificate
A notarial act shall be evidenced by a **certificate**.

QUICK QUESTIONS

RULONA 315
T?F? A notarial certificate does not have to be executed contemporaneously with the performance of the notarial act.

RULONA 315
A notarial certificate must be signed and _____ by the notarial officer.

RULONA 315
A notarial certificate must identify the county and _____ in which the notarial act is performed.

RULONA 315
A notarial certificate must contain the _____ of the notarial officer.

RULONA 315
The certificate of a notary must indicate the date of _____ of the notarial officer's commission.

ANSWERS

False

A notarial certificate <u>MUST</u> be executed contemporaneously with the performance of the notarial act.

dated

A notarial certificate must be signed and **dated** by the notarial officer.

state

A notarial certificate must identify the county and **State** in which the notarial act is performed. (Note also RULONA Regulations 167.71: State of Pennsylvania OR Commonwealth of Pennsylvania may be used.)

title

A notarial certificate must contain the **title** of the notarial officer.

expiration

The certificate of a notary must indicate the date of **expiration** of the notarial officer's commission.

QUICK QUESTIONS

RULONA 315
If a notarial act regarding a tangible record is performed by a notary public, an official stamp (may / shall) be affixed to the certificate.

RULONA 315
If a notarial act regarding a tangible record is performed by other than a notary public, an official stamp (may / shall) be affixed to the certificate.

RULONA 315
If a notarial act regarding an electronic record is performed by a notary public or other than a notary public, an official stamp (may / shall) be attached to or logically associated with the certificate.

RULONA 315
A notarial officer (may / may not) affix the notarial officer's signature to or logically associate it with a certificate until the notarial act has been performed.

RULONA 315
If a notarial act is performed regarding a tangible record, does a certificate have to be a part of or attached to the record?

ANSWERS

shall

If a notarial act regarding a tangible record is performed by a notary public, an official stamp **shall** be affixed to the certificate.

may

If a notarial act regarding a tangible record is performed by a notary public, an official stamp **may** be affixed to the certificate.

may

If a notarial act regarding an electronic record is performed by a notary public or other than a notary public, an official stamp **may** be attached to or logically associated with the certificate.

may not

A notarial officer **may not** affix the notarial officer's signature to or logically associate it with a certificate until the notarial act has been performed.

Yes

If a notarial act is performed regarding a tangible record, a certificate shall be part of or securely attached to the record. If a notarial act is performed regarding an electronic record, the certificate shall be affixed to or logically associated with the electronic record.

QUICK QUESTIONS

http://www.dos.pa.gov
The Revised Uniform Law on Notarial Acts (RULONA) requires that a notarial act must be evidenced by a

_____ .

http://www.dos.pa.gov
T/F? It is never acceptable for a notary to place one's signature and seal on a document, without any notarial language.

RULONA 317
The seal (may / must) be capable of being copied together with the record to which it is affixed or attached or with which it is logically associated.

RULONA 318
Who is responsible for the security of the stamping device of the notary public?

RULONA 318
May a notary public allow a trusted friend to use the stamping device to perform a notarial act?

ANSWERS

certificate

The Revised Uniform Law on Notarial Acts (RULONA) requires that a notarial act must be evidenced by a **certificate**.

True

The notary public must include a statement indicating the type of notarial act performed, showing when, where and before whom the notarial act was completed. It is never acceptable to place only one's signature and seal on a document, without any notarial language.

must

The seal **must** be capable of being copied together with the record to which it is affixed or attached or with which it is logically associated.

notary public

The **notary public** is responsible for the security of the stamping device of the notary public

No

A notary public may <u>not</u> allow another individual to use the stamping device to perform a notarial act.

QUICK QUESTIONS

RULONA 318
On resignation of a notary public commission or on the expiration of the date set forth in the stamping device, the notary public shall disable the stamping device by destroying, defacing, damaging, erasing or securing it against use in a manner which renders it _____.

RULONA 318
An individual whose notary commission has been suspended or revoked shall surrender possession of the stamping device to the _____.

RULONA 319
A notary public shall maintain a journal in which the notary public records in _____ order all notarial acts that the notary public performs.

RULONA 319
A journal may be created on a tangible medium or in an _____ format.

RULONA 319
If the journal is maintained on a tangible medium, it shall be a bound register with _____ pages.

ANSWERS

unusable

On resignation of a notary public commission or on the expiration of the date set forth in the stamping device, the notary public shall disable the stamping device by destroying, defacing, damaging, erasing or securing it against use in a manner which renders it **unusable**.

department

An individual whose notary commission has been suspended or revoked shall surrender possession of the stamping device to the **department**.

chronological

A notary public shall maintain a journal in which the notary public records in **chronological** order all notarial acts that the notary public performs.

electronic

A journal may be created on a tangible medium or in an **electronic** format.

numbered

If the journal is maintained on a tangible medium, it shall be a bound register with **numbered** pages.

QUICK QUESTIONS

RULONA 319
On death or incompetency of a notary public, the personal representative or guardian shall deliver the notary journal within ___ days to the office of recorder of deeds in county where notary maintained his office.

RULONA 319
T/F? A journal and each public record of the notary public are exempt from execution.

RULONA 319
A notary public shall give a _____ copy of the journal to a person that applies for it.

RULONA 319
A journal (may / may not) be used by any person other than the notary public.

RULONA 319
A journal (may / may not) be surrendered to an employer of the notary public upon termination of employment.

ANSWERS

30

On death or incompetency of a notary public, the personal representative or guardian shall deliver the notary journal within **30** days to the office of recorder of deeds in county where notary maintained his office.

True

A journal and each public record of the notary public are exempt from execution. A journal is the exclusive property of the notary.

certified

A notary public shall give a **certified** copy of the journal to a person that applies for it.

may not

A journal **may not** be used by any person other than the notary public.

may not

A journal **may not** be surrendered to an employer of the notary public upon termination of employment.

QUICK QUESTIONS

RULONA 320

Before a notary performs the initial notarial act with respect to an electronic record, a notary public shall notify the _____ that the notary will be performing notarial acts with respect to electronic records and identify each technology the notary intends to use.

RULONA 321

An applicant for appointment and commission as a notary public must be at least ____ years of age.

RULONA 321

An applicant for appointment and commission as a notary public must be a citizen or _____ of the United States.

RULONA 321

An applicant for appointment and commission as a notary public must be a resident or have a place of employment in

_____.

RULONA 321

An applicant for appointment and commission as a notary public must be able to read and write _____.

ANSWERS

department

Before a notary performs the initial notarial act with respect to an electronic record, a notary public shall notify the **department** that the notary will be performing notarial acts with respect to electronic records and identify each technology the notary intends to use.

18

An applicant for appointment and commission as a notary public must be at least **18** years of age.

permanent legal resident

An applicant for appointment and commission as a notary public must be a citizen or **permanent legal resident** of the United States.

this Commonwealth

An applicant for appointment and commission as a notary public must be a resident or have a place of employment in **this Commonwealth**.

English

An applicant for appointment and commission as a notary public must be able to read and write **English**.

QUICK QUESTIONS

RULONA 321
A notary public application must be accompanied by a nonrefundable fee of $____, payable to the Commonwealth of Pennsylvania. This amount shall include the application fee for notary public commission and fee for filing of the bond with the department.

RULONA 321
Within 45 days after appointment and before issuance of a commission as a notary public, the applicant must obtain a surety bond in the amount of $_____ or the amount set by regulation of the department.

RULONA 321
T/F? If a notary public violates law with respect to notaries public in this Commonwealth, the surety or issuing entity is liable under the bond.

RULONA 321
The surety or issuing entity must give ___ days' notice to the department before canceling the bond.

RULONA 321
A notary public may perform notarial acts in this Commonwealth only during the period in which a _____ is on file with the department.

ANSWERS

$42

A notary public application must be accompanied by a nonrefundable fee of **$42**, payable to the Commonwealth of Pennsylvania. This amount shall include the application fee for notary public commission and fee for filing of the bond with the department.

$10,000

Within 45 days after appointment and before issuance of a commission as a notary public, the applicant must obtain a surety bond in the amount of **$10,000** or the amount set by regulation of the department.

True

If a notary public violates law with respect to notaries public in this Commonwealth, the surety or issuing entity is liable under the bond.

30

The surety or issuing entity must give **30** days' notice to the department before canceling the bond.
Also, the surety or issuing entity shall notify the department not later than 30 days after making a payment to a claimant under the bond.

valid bond

A notary public may perform notarial acts in this Commonwealth only during the period in which a **valid bond** is on file with the department.

QUICK QUESTIONS

RULONA 321
The official signature of each notary public shall be registered, for a fee of 50¢, in the "Notary Register" provided for that purpose in the _____ office of the county where the notary public maintains an office.

RULONA 321
The official signature of each notary public shall be registered within: (i) _____ days after appointment or reappointment; and (ii) _____ days after moving to a different county.

RULONA 321
In a county of the second class, the official signature of each notary public shall be registered in the office of

_____.

RULONA 321
Upon appointment and prior to entering into the duties of a notary public, the bond, oath of office and commission must be recorded in the office of the recorder of deeds of the county in which the notary public _____.

RULONA 321
Within ___ days of recording the bond, oath of office and commission in the office of the recorder of deeds, a copy of the bond and oath of office must be filed with the department.

ANSWERS

prothonotary's
The official signature of each notary public shall be registered, for a fee of 50¢, in the "Notary Register" provided for that purpose in the **prothonotary's** office of the county where the notary public maintains an office.

45....30
The official signature of each notary public shall be registered within: (i) **45** days after appointment or reappointment; and (ii) **30** days after moving to a different county.

the clerk of courts

In a county of the second class, the official signature of each notary public shall be registered in the office of **the clerk of courts**.

maintains an office
Upon appointment and prior to entering into the duties of a notary public, the bond, oath of office and commission must be recorded in the office of the recorder of deeds of the county in which the notary public **maintains an office**.

90
Within **90** days of recording the bond, oath of office and commission in the office of the recorder of deeds, a copy of the bond and oath of office must be filed with the department.

QUICK QUESTIONS

RULONA 321
A commission to act as a notary public (does / does not) not provide a notary public any immunity or benefit conferred by law of this Commonwealth on public officials or employees.

RULONA 322
A notary public applicant must, within the ___-month period immediately preceding application, complete a course of at least ___ hours of notary public basic education approved by the department.

RULONA 323
T/F? The department may impose sanctions for failure to comply with RULONA.

RULONA 323
An act which may result in sanctions of a notary public include conviction of a _____.

RULONA 323
T/F? An act which may result in sanctions of a notary public include conviction of any offense.

ANSWERS

does not

A commission to act as a notary public **does not** provide a notary public any immunity or benefit conferred by law of this Commonwealth on public officials or employees.

6....3

A notary public applicant must, within the **6**-month period immediately preceding application, complete a course of at least **3** hours of notary public basic education approved by the department. (Also applies to a renewal application.)

True

The department may impose sanctions for failure to comply with RULONA. Sanctions include denial, refusal to renew, suspend, reprimand or impose a condition on a commission as notary public

felony

An act which may result in sanctions of a notary public include conviction of a **felony** (or acceptance of Accelerated Rehabilitative Disposition for a felony or an offense involving fraud, dishonesty or deceit.)

False

An act which may result in sanctions of a notary public include conviction of any felony or other specified offenses.

QUICK QUESTIONS

RULONA 323
T/F? The department may deny a notary public commission if the applicant was denied a notary public commission in another state.

RULONA 323
The department may impose an administrative penalty of up to $_____ on a notary public for each act or omission which constitutes a violation of RULONA.

RULONA 323
T/F? A person may seek and obtain civil remedies against notaries public.

RULONA 323
T/F? Pretending to be a notary or a notarial officer and performing any action in furtherance of such false pretense shall subject the person to the penalties set forth in 18 Pa.C.S. § 4913 (relating to impersonating a notary public or a holder of a professional or occupational license).

RULONA 324
The database of notaries public verifies the authority of a notary public and indicates whether a notary public has notified the department that the notary public will be performing notarial acts on _____ records.

ANSWERS

True

Also may be denied for refusal to renew, revocation, suspension or conditioning of a notary public commission in another state.

$1,000

The department may impose an administrative penalty of up to **$1,000** on a notary public for each act or omission which constitutes a violation of RULONA. (May also be imposed on any person who performs a notarial act without being properly appointed and commissioned.

True

A person may also seek criminal penalties.

True

18 Pa.C.S. § 4913: Generally, a misdemeanor of the first or second degree. It includes use of an official stamp by a person who is not a notary.

electronic

The database of notaries public verifies the authority of a notary public and indicates whether a notary public has notified the department that the notary public will be performing notarial acts on **electronic** records.

QUICK QUESTIONS

RULONA 325
A commission as a notary public (does / does not) authorize the notary public to assist persons in drafting legal records, give legal advice or otherwise practice law.

RULONA 325
A commission as a notary public (does / does not) authorize the notary to act as an immigration consultant or an expert on immigration matters.

RULONA 325
A commission as notary public (does / does not) authorize the notary to represent a person in a judicial or administrative proceeding relating to immigration to the United States, or United States citizenship.

RULONA 325
A notary public who is not an attorney (may / may not) use the term "notario" or "notario publico".

RULONA 325
T/F? A notary public may advertise that he offers notarial services.

ANSWERS

does not

A commission as a notary public **does not** not authorize the notary public to assist persons in drafting legal records, give legal advice or otherwise practice law.

does not

A commission as a notary public **does not** authorize the notary to act as an immigration consultant or an expert on immigration matters.

does not

A commission as notary public **does not** authorize the notary to represent a person in a judicial or administrative proceeding relating to immigration to the United States, or United States citizenship.

may not

A notary public who is not an attorney **may not** use the term "notario" or "notario publico".

True

A notary public **may** advertise that he offers notarial services. In such a case, the notary must include in the advertisement a required prescribed statement regarding the limits of the services and that the notary is not an attorney. (Does not apply to attorneys.)

QUICK QUESTIONS

RULONA 326
The failure of a notarial officer to perform a duty or meet a requirement specified in this chapter (does / does not) invalidate a notarial act performed by the notarial officer.

RULONA 327
The department (may / may not) promulgate rules to implement the RULONA.

RULONA 327
Who establishes the process for approving and accepting surety bonds under section 321(d) (relating to appointment and commission as notary)?

RULONA 327
T/F? The department provides for administration of the examination under section 322(a) (relating to examination, basic education and continuing education) and course of study under section 322(b).

RULONA 327
The department may require applicants for appointment and commission as notaries public to submit _____ history record information as provided in 18 Pa.C.S. Ch. 91.

ANSWERS

does not

The failure of a notarial officer to perform a duty or meet a requirement specified in this chapter **does not** invalidate a notarial act performed by the notarial officer.

may

The department **may** promulgate rules to implement the RULONA.

the department

The department establishes the process for approving and accepting surety bonds under section 321(d) (relating to appointment and commission as notary).

True

The department also requires applicants for appointment and commission as notaries public to submit criminal history record information as provided in 18 Pa.C.S. Ch. 91 (relating to criminal history record information) as a condition of employment.

criminal

The department may require applicants for appointment and commission as notaries public to submit **criminal** history record information as provided in 18 Pa.C.S. Ch. 91.

QUICK QUESTIONS

NOTARIES PUBLIC (57 PA.C.S.) - OMNIBUS AMENDMENTS
Act of Jul. 9, 2014, P.L. 1035, No. 119 Cl. 57 Session of 2014 No. 2014-119

An application for a commission as a notary public shall be accompanied by a nonrefundable fee of $__ , payable to the Commonwealth of Pennsylvania (fee for notary public commission and fee for filing of bond with the department).

NOTARIES PUBLIC (57 PA.C.S.) - OMNIBUS AMENDMENTS
Act of Jul. 9, 2014, P.L. 1035, No. 119 Cl. 57 Session of 2014 No. 2014-119

Section 321: Within __ days after appointment or reappointment, and prior to entering into the duties of a notary public, the bond, oath of office and commission must be recorded in the office of the recorder of deeds of the county in which the notary public maintains an office.

NOTARIES PUBLIC (57 PA.C.S.) - OMNIBUS AMENDMENTS
Act of Jul. 9, 2014, P.L. 1035, No. 119 Cl. 57 Session of 2014 No. 2014-119

Section 321: Within __ days of recording of the bond, oath of office and commission, a copy of the bond and oath of office must be filed with the department.

Uniform Acknowledgment Act - Section 6

T/F? An acknowledgment of a married woman may be made in the same form as though she were unmarried.

Uniform Acknowledgment Act - Section 8

The certificate of the acknowledging officer shall be completed by his signature, his official seal, if he has one, the title of his office, and, if he is a notary public, the date his _____ expires.

ANSWERS

NOTARIES PUBLIC (57 PA.C.S.) - OMNIBUS AMENDMENTS
Act of Jul. 9, 2014, P.L. 1035, No. 119 Cl. 57 Session of 2014 No. 2014-119

An application for a commission as a notary public shall be accompanied by a nonrefundable fee of **$42**, payable to the Commonwealth of Pennsylvania (fee for notary public commission and fee for filing of bond with the department).

NOTARIES PUBLIC (57 PA.C.S.) - OMNIBUS AMENDMENTS
Act of Jul. 9, 2014, P.L. 1035, No. 119 Cl. 57 Session of 2014 No. 2014-119

Within **45** days after appointment or reappointment, and prior to entering into the duties of a notary public, the bond, oath of office and commission must be recorded in the office of the recorder of deeds of the county in which the notary public maintains an office.

NOTARIES PUBLIC (57 PA.C.S.) - OMNIBUS AMENDMENTS
Act of Jul. 9, 2014, P.L. 1035, No. 119 Cl. 57 Session of 2014 No. 2014-119

Within **90** days of recording of the bond, oath of office and commission, a copy of the bond and oath of office must be filed with the department.

True
Marriage status does not change the form of an acknowledgment.

commission
The certificate of the acknowledging officer shall be completed by his signature, his official seal, if he has one, the title of his office, and, if he is a notary public, the date his **commission** expires.

QUICK QUESTIONS

Uniform Acknowledgment Act - Section 9

T/F? If the acknowledgment is taken within this State, or if taken without this State by an officer of this State, or is made without the United States by an officer of the United States, no authentication shall be necessary.

Uniform Acknowledgment Act - Section 10.1

Persons serving with Armed Forces of the US or their dependents may acknowledge the same before any commissioned officer in active service of the armed forces of the US with the rank of _____ or higher.

http://www.dos.pa.gov

The fee for taking an acknowledgment is _____ .

http://www.dos.pa.gov

The fee for taking an acknowledgment (each additional name) is _____ .

http://www.dos.pa.gov

The fee for administering oath or affirmation (per individual taking oath or affirmation) is _____ .

ANSWERS

True

If acknowledgment is taken outside Pennsylvania, but in the US, a territory or insular possession of the US, or the District of Columbia, no authentication is necessary if the official before whom the acknowledgment is taken affixes his official seal to the instrument so acknowledged.

Second Lieutenant

Persons serving with Armed Forces of the US or their dependents may acknowledge the same before any commissioned officer in active service of the armed forces of the US with the rank of **Second Lieutenant** or higher.

$ 5

The fee for taking an acknowledgment is **$ 5**.

$ 2

The fee for taking an acknowledgment (each additional name) is **$ 2**.

$ 5

The fee for administering oath or affirmation (per individual taking oath or affirmation) is **$ 5**.

QUICK QUESTIONS

---

http://www.dos.pa.gov

The fee for taking verification on oath or affirmation (no matter how many signatures) is $_____.

---

http://www.dos.pa.gov

The fee for witnessing or attesting a signature (per signature) is $_____.

---

http://www.dos.pa.gov

The fee for certifying or attesting a copy or deposition (per certified copy) is $_____.

---

http://www.dos.pa.gov

The fee for noting a protest of a negotiable instrument (per page) is $_____.

---

http://www.dos.pa.gov

Notaries may only charge fees as set by the _____.

ANSWERS

$ 5

The fee for taking verification on oath or affirmation (no matter how many signatures) is **$ 5**.

$ 5

The fee for witnessing or attesting a signature (per signature) is **$ 5**.

$ 5

The fee for certifying or attesting a copy or deposition (per certified copy) is **$ 5**.

$ 3

The fee for noting a protest of a negotiable instrument (per page) is **$ 3**.

Department of State.

Notaries may only charge fees as set by the **Department of State**.

QUICK QUESTIONS

http://www.dos.pa.gov

Fees must be _____ stated.

---

http://www.dos.pa.gov

List of Fees must be displayed (if notary charges fees). In the alternative, notary may _____ .

---

http://www.dos.pa.gov

T/F? Fees may be waived by notaries.

---

http://www.dos.pa.gov

Fees are the property of the _____ (and not the employer) unless the notary and employer enter into a different agreement.

---

http://www.dos.pa.gov

Notaries may charge clerical and administrative fees and customers should be informed _____ to notarization.

ANSWERS

separately

Fees must be **separately** stated.

provide a list of fees to person requesting it.

List of Fees must be displayed (if notary charges fees). In the alternative, notary may **provide a list of fees to person requesting it**.

True

Fees may be waived by notaries.

notary

Fees are the property of the **notary** (and not the employer) unless the notary and employer enter into a different agreement.

prior

Notaries may charge clerical and administrative fees and customers should be informed **prior** to notarization.

QUICK QUESTIONS

RULONA Regulations 161.2

A notary public (may / may not) charge any fee for notarizing the supporting affidavit required in an Emergency Absentee Ballot or the affidavit of a person needing assistance to vote an absentee ballot.

RULONA Regulations 167.11

If a notary applicant is not a resident of Pennsylvania, the applicant must have a place of employment or practice in

_____.

RULONA Regulations 167.13

If a notary public neither resides nor works in the Commonwealth, he is deemed to have resigned from the office of notary public and must notify the Department within ___ days of the effective date of resignation.

RULONA Regulations 167.14 (d)

If an applicant's preferred signature is not legible and recognizable, what must the applicant do?

RULONA Regulations 167.18

Notary public must notify Department of State within ___ days of any change in the information on file with the Department.

ANSWERS

may not

A notary public **may not** charge any fee for notarizing the supporting affidavit required in an Emergency Absentee Ballot or the affidavit of a person needing assistance to vote an absentee ballot.

this Commonwealth

If a notary applicant is not a resident of Pennsylvania, the applicant must have a place of employment or practice in **this Commonwealth.** (A post office box number is not a sufficient address for Department of State records.)

30

If a notary public neither resides nor works in the Commonwealth, he is deemed to have resigned from the office of notary public and must notify the Department within **30** days of the effective date of resignation.

If an applicant's preferred signature is not legible and recognizable, **the applicant must also legibly print his or her name immediately adjacent to his or her preferred signature**.

30

Notary public must notify Department of State within **30** days of any change in the information on file with the Department.

QUICK QUESTIONS

RULONA Regulations 167.21

167.22 d) Notification of loss or theft of stamping device under section 318(b) shall be made in writing or electronically to the Department within ___ days after the date the notary public or personal representative or guardian discovers that the stamping device was lost, misplaced, stolen or is otherwise unavailable.

RULONA Regulations 167.21
A notary journal (may / may not) contain any personal financial or identification information about the notary's clients, such as complete Social Security numbers, complete drivers' license numbers or complete account numbers.

RULONA Regulations 167.21

If a fee is waived or not charged, the notary public shall indicate this fact in the journal entry, using

_____.

RULONA Regulations 167.21

Each page of the notary journal shall be _____ numbered from the beginning to the end of the journal.

RULONA Regulations 167.41

T/F? Neither initials alone nor nicknames will be accepted on the application or as part of the signature required on a notarial act.

ANSWERS

10
Notification of loss or theft of stamping device under section 318(b) shall be made in writing or electronically to the Department within **10** days after the date the notary public or personal representative or guardian discovers that the stamping device was lost, misplaced, stolen or is otherwise unavailable.

may not
A notary journal **may not** contain any personal financial or identification information about the notary's clients, such as complete Social Security numbers, complete drivers' license numbers or complete account numbers.

If a fee is waived or not charged, the notary public shall indicate this fact in the journal entry, using **"n/c" or "0" (zero) or a similar notation**.

consecutively
Each page of the notary journal shall be **consecutively** numbered from the beginning to the end of the journal.

True
Neither initials alone nor nicknames will be accepted on the application or as part of the signature required on a notarial act. Also, the name of a notary <u>MAY</u> include suffixes (Junior, Senior, etc.) but <u>MAY NOT</u> include prefixes such a "Doctor", "Reverend", etc.

QUICK QUESTIONS

RULONA Regulations 167.41

The certificate of notarial act must be worded and completed using only letters, characters and a language that are read, written and understood by

_____.

RULONA Regulations 167.48
A notarial officer may perform a notarial act on a document that is a translation of a document if the person performing the translation signs a _____ stating that the translation is accurate and complete.

RULONA Regulations 167.50

A notary public (may / may not) perform a notarial act with respect to a record which is designed to provide information within blank spaces.

RULONA Regulations 167.61
T/F? A record may be signed in the notarial officer's presence or a record may be signed prior to the acknowledgment.

RULONA Regulations 167.71
T/F? For purposes of attaching a notarial certificate to a tangible record, securely attached means stapled, grommeted or otherwise bound to the tangible record.

ANSWERS

the notarial officer

The certificate of notarial act must be worded and completed using only letters, characters and a language that are read, written and understood by **the notarial officer**.

A notarial officer may perform a notarial act on a document that is a translation of a document if the person performing the translation signs a **verification on oath or affirmation** stating that the translation is accurate and complete.

---

may not

A notary public **may not** perform a notarial act with respect to a record which is designed to provide information within blank spaces.

True

A record may be signed in the notarial officer's presence or a record may be signed prior to the acknowledgment.

(A record may not be signed subsequent to an acknowledgment.)

True

For purposes of attaching a notarial certificate to a tangible record, securely attached means stapled, grommeted or otherwise bound to the tangible record.
(Securely attached does not include the use of tape, paperclips or binder clips.)

QUICK QUESTIONS

RULONA Regulations 167.81
A notary public who wishes to perform notarial acts with respect to electronic records shall be authorized by the _____ to act as an "electronic notary" or "e-notary" prior to performing notarial acts with respect to electronic records.

RULONA Regulations 167.82

T/F? All requirements of a notarial act performed with respect to a tangible record apply to an electronic record.

RULONA Regulations 167.65
TF? If a record is intended to be sent overseas and requires an apostille or certification from the U.S. Department of State or Pennsylvania Department of State, the record must be certified by office where original or official copy of record is maintained or by the public official who issued the record.

RULONA Regulations 167.124

T/F? A notary may not notarize his or her own signature or statement or a spouse's signature or statement, notarize records in blank, or post-date or pre-date notarial acts.

RULONA Regulations 167.126

T/F? No person who represents himself in a legal matter shall be considered to have engaged in the unauthorized practice of law.

ANSWERS

A notary public who wishes to perform notarial acts with respect to electronic records shall be authorized by the **Department** to act as an "electronic notary" or "e-notary" prior to performing notarial acts with respect to electronic records.

True

All requirements of a notarial act performed with respect to a tangible record apply to an electronic record. (This includes personal appearance and identification of the individual appearing before the notary public, completion of a notarial certificate, use of an official stamp and recording of the notarial act in the notary journal).

True

Examples include deeds, marriage records, court orders and corporate documents filed with a state office or state repository as the official record.

True

Also a notary may not alter a document after it has been notarized, fail to require physical presence of an individual, make a statement in or executing a signature on a record, or fail to have personal knowledge or satisfactory evidence of the identity of an individual appearing before the notary.

True

No person who represents himself in a legal matter shall be considered to have engaged in the unauthorized practice of law.

MULTIPLE CHOICE QUESTIONS

Which of the following is not listed as a notarial act in RULONA 302?

A. taking an acknowledgment
B. administering an oath or affirmation
C. witnessing or attesting a signature
D. testifying on a civil jury

A "Person." (RULONA 302) does not include:

A. Any individual
B. A government or governmental subdivision, agency or instrumentality.
C. A trained pet.
D. Any other legal or commercial entity.

In which of the following cases is a notary prohibited from performing a notarial act? In all cases where:

A. notary is a shareholder of a publicly traded company that is a party to the transaction.
B. the notarial officer's wife has a pecuniary interest
C. notary is an employee of a corporate party
D. fee of notary is not contingent on the transaction

ANSWERS

D. testifying on a civil jury
(RULONA 302)

Other <u>valid</u> notarial acts include:
• taking a verification on oath or affirmation
• certifying or attesting a copy or deposition
• noting a protest of a negotiable instrument.

C. A trained pet
(RULONA 302)

"Person" also includes "corporation, business trust, statutory trust, estate, trust, partnership, limited liability company, association, joint venture or public corporation."

B. the notarial officer's wife has a pecuniary interest
(RULONA 304)

A notarial officer may not perform a notarial act with respect to a record in which the notarial officer or the notarial officer's spouse has a direct or pecuniary interest.

MULTIPLE CHOICE QUESTIONS

Specified satisfactory evidence includes all of the following, except:

A. a passport
B. a driver's license
C. nondriver identification card
D. an IRS W-2 form

If the notary determines that the individual's signature on the record or statement does not conform to the signature on a form of identification used to determine the identity of the individual; the notary public:
A. can accept either signature.
B. can charge a higher fee because of the default.
C. may not question the identity.
D. may refuse to perform the notarial act.

Which of the following is not correct? A notarial act may be performed in this Commonwealth by:
A. A judge of a court of record.
B. A clerk, deputy clerk of a court having a seal.
C. A recorder of deeds or deputy recorder of deeds.
D. Any pharmacist employed by a large chain.

ANSWERS

D. an IRS W-2 form
(RULONA 307)

Any government ID not specified in RULONA 307 must be: (A) is current; (B) contains the signature or a photograph of the individual; and (C) is satisfactory to the notarial officer.

D. may refuse to perform the notarial act
(RULONA 308)

A notarial officer **may refuse to perform a notarial act** if the notarial officer is not satisfied that the individual's signature on the record or statement substantially conforms to the signature on a form of identification used to determine the identity of the individual.

D. Any pharmacist employed by a large chain.
(RULONA 310)

(The pharmacist must be a commissioned notary public) A notarial act may also be performed by a prothonotary or deputy prothonotary (Chief Clerk and Deputy Chief Clerk involved with non-criminal court records such as property deeds and marriage licenses.)

MULTIPLE CHOICE QUESTIONS

Which of the following is not specifically authorized to perform notarial acts?

A. a notary public
B. a member of the major judiciary
C. certain clerks of recorder of deeds
D. an individual authorized by law

Which of the following is not correct? A notarial certificate:

A. must be executed contemporaneously with the performance of the notarial act.
B. be signed and dated by the notarial officer.
C. must state the country in which executed.
D. must contain the title of the notarial officer.

Which of the following is not a short form certificate of notarial action?

A. Verification on oath or affirmation
B. Witnessing or attesting a signature
C. Certifying a reconstructed record as a true copy.
D. Certifying the transcript of a deposition

ANSWERS

B. a member of the major judiciary
(RULONA 310)

The correct answer is: a member of the **minor** judiciary.

C. must state the country in which executed
(RULONA 315)

The notarial certificate must identify the **county and State** in which the notarial act is performed;

C. Certifying a reconstructed record as a true copy.
(RULONA 316)

This should read: "Certifying a **copy** of a record".
Other valid short form certificates are:
(1) Acknowledgment in an individual capacity
(2) Acknowledgment in a representative capacity
(3) Acknowledgment by an attorney at law

MULTIPLE CHOICE QUESTIONS

Which of the following do not apply to the official stamp of a notary public?

A. The words "Commonwealth of Pennsylvania"
B. The words "Navy Seal".
C. County where notary public maintains his office.
D. Date notary public's commission expires.

Which of the following do not apply to the official stamp of a notary public?

A. The name as it appears on the commission of the notary public and the words "Notary Public."
B. The words "Notary Seal."
C. The date the notary public's commission expires.
D. The date of birth of the notary.

Which is not correct? A notary journal entry contains:

A. Date and time of notarial act
B. Description of record, if any, and type of notarial act.
C. Initials and address of each individual for whom notarial act is performed.
D. If identity of individual is based on personal knowledge, a statement to that effect.

ANSWERS

B. The words "Navy Seal"
(RULONA 317)

This should read, "**Notary** Seal".

D. The date of birth of the notary
(RULONA 317)

The date of birth of the notary is <u>not</u> a requirement on the official stamp.

C. Initials and address of each individual for whom notarial act is performed.
(RULONA 319)

This should read: The <u>full name</u> and address of each individual for whom notarial act is performed.

MULTIPLE CHOICE QUESTIONS

If a notary resigns or his commission is revoked, he shall deliver the journal of the notary public to the office of the recorder of deeds in the county where the notary public last maintained an office within _____ days of resignation or revocation of commission.
A. 10
B. 30
C. 45
D. 60

A notary public may advertise or represent that the notary public may:
A. assist persons in drafting legal records.
B. give legal advice.
C. practice law.
D. perform notarial duties

Which of the following is not correct? The acknowledgment of any instrument within this state may be made before:
A. judge of a court of record.
B. clerk, prothonotary or deputy prothonotary.
C. deputy clerk of a court having a seal.
D. a secretary of an attorney.

ANSWERS

B. 30
(RULONA 319)

If a notary resigns or his commission is revoked, he shall deliver the journal of the notary public to the office of the recorder of deeds in the county where the notary public last maintained an office within **30** days of resignation or revocation of commission.

D. perform notarial duties
(RULONA 325)

A notary public may not advertise or represent that the notary public may assist persons in drafting legal records, give legal advice or practice law.

D. a secretary of an attorney
(Uniform Acknowledgment Act - Section 2

A secretary of an attorney is not correct because the choice does not state that the secretary is a commissioned notary public.

MULTIPLE CHOICE QUESTIONS

Which of the following is not correct? The acknowledgment of any instrument within this state may be made before a:
A. recorder of deeds or deputy recorder of deeds
B. bank supervisor
C. notary public
D. justice of the peace, magistrate or alderman

Which of the following is not correct?
The acknowledgment of any instrument may be made without the State, but within the United States by:
A. a clerk or deputy of any federal court;
B. a federal employee in good standing
C. a clerk, prothonotary or deputy prothonotary or deputy clerk of any court of record of any state or other jurisdiction;
C. a notary public, a recorder of deeds.

Which of the following is not correct?
The acknowledgment of any instrument may be made outside the US before:
A. an ambassador, minister, charge d' affaires, consul, commercial attaché
B. a notary public of country where acknowledgment is made;
C. an official interpreter
D. a judge or clerk of a court of record of the country where acknowledgment is made.

ANSWERS

B. bank supervisor
(Uniform Acknowledgment Act - Section 2

A bank supervisor is not correct because the choice does not state that the bank supervisor is a commissioned notary public.

B. a federal employee in good standing
(Uniform Acknowledgment Act - Section 3

A "federal employee in good standing" is not correct because the choice does not state that the person is a commissioned notary public.

C. an official interpreter
(Uniform Acknowledgment Act - Section 4

An official interpreter is not listed as an authorized official.

ACE THE PENNSYLVANIA NOTARY PUBLIC EXAM QUESTIONS AND ANSWERS

MULTIPLE CHOICE QUESTIONS

Which of the following is eligible to hold the office of notary public?

A. judge of a higher court.
B. member of Congress.
C. the head of a Pennsylvania state department
D. a druggist who qualifies for the office

The seal shall have a maximum height of
_____, with a plain border.

A. (.5) inch and width of two and one-half (2 1/2)
B. (1.5) inch and width of three and one-half (3 1/2)
C. (1) inch and width of three and one-half (3 1/2)
D. (2) inch and width of four and one-half (4 1/2)

Which of the following is not correct?
A notary is not required to use an electronic seal, if the following information is attached to the electronic signature or electronic record being notarized, acknowledged or verified:
A. The full name of the notary along with the words "Notary Public."
B. The name of the county in which the notary maintains an office.
C. The date the notary's commission is due to expire.
D. The brand name of the electronic device being employed.

83

ANSWERS

D. a druggist who qualifies for the office
(Notary Public Law: Section 4)

(1) Any person holding any judicial office in this Commonwealth, except the office of justice of the peace, magistrate, or alderman.
(2) Every member of Congress, and any person, whether an officer, a subordinate officer, or agent, holding any office or appointment of profit or trust under the legislative, executive, or judiciary departments of the government of the United States, to which a salary, fees or perquisites are attached.

C. (1) inch and width of three and one-half (3 1/2)
(Notary Public Law: Section 12)

The seal shall be stamped in a prominent place on the official notarial certificate near the notary's signature in such a manner as to be capable of photographic reproduction.

D. The brand name of the electronic device being employed.
(Notary Public Law: Section 12)

MULTIPLE CHOICE QUESTIONS

Which of the following is not correct?
Notaries have power to:

A. administer oaths
B. certify copies
C. take affidavits
D. interrogate witnesses during a trial

Which of the following is not correct?
Notaries have power to:

A. administer affirmations
B. take depositions
C. adjudge a person in contempt
D. take verifications

Which of the following regarding notary fees is not correct?
A. Fees of notaries shall be fixed by the Secretary with approval of the Attorney General.
B. A notary shall not charge a fee in excess of fees fixed by the Secretary.
C. Fees of notaries public shall be displayed in a conspicuous location in the notary's place of business or provided upon request to any person utilizing the services of the notary.
D. A notary may charge a greater fee for time-consuming cases.

ANSWERS

D. interrogate witnesses during a trial
(Notary Public Law: Section 16)

C. adjudge a person in contempt
(Notary Public Law: Section 16)

D. A notary may charge a greater fee for time-consuming cases.
(Notary Public Law: Section 21)

MULTIPLE CHOICE QUESTIONS

Which of the following regarding notary fees is <u>not</u> correct?

A. The fees of the notary shall be separately stated.
B. A notary public may waive the right to charge a fee, in which case the fees do not have to be displayed.
C. A notary fee charged by an attorney may be double the statutory fee.
D. The fee for any notary public employed by a bank or banking institution shall be the property of the notary.

The jurisdiction of notaries public is coextensive with the boundaries of the _____.

A. United States
B. North America
C. Commonwealth
D. county where principal office is located

Any person who is a notary public and who resides outside this Commonwealth shall be deemed to have irrevocably appointed the _____ as the person's agent upon whom may be served any summons, subpoena, order or other process.

A. clerk of the county
B. public attorney
C. Comptroller of the Commonwealth
D. Secretary of the Commonwealth

ANSWERS

C. A notary fee charged by an attorney may be double the statutory fee.
(Notary Public Law Section 21)

C. Commonwealth

The jurisdiction of notaries public is coextensive with the boundaries of the **Commonwealth**.

D. Secretary of the Commonwealth
(Notary Public Law: Section 3)

Any person who is a notary public and who resides outside this Commonwealth shall be deemed to have irrevocably appointed **Secretary of the Commonwealth** as the person's agent upon whom may be served any summons, subpoena, order or other process.

MULTIPLE CHOICE QUESTIONS

A notary applicant must complete at least ___ hours of approved notary education within the ___ month period immediately preceding their application.

A. 6....3
B. 3....3
C. 3...12
D. 3....6

An applicant for notary public shall not have been convicted of or pled guilty or "nolo contendere" to a _____ or a lesser offense incompatible with the duties of a notary public during the ____ year period preceding the date of the application.

A. offense....3
B. felony....5
C. misdemeanor....3
D. petty offense....5

Application for Reappointment to the office of notary public shall be filed at least ___ months prior to the expiration of the commission under which the notary is acting.

A. 2
B. 3
C. 4
D. 6

ANSWERS

D. 3....6
(Notary Public Law: Section 5)

A notary applicant must complete at least **3** hours of approved notary education within the **6**-month period immediately preceding their application.

B. felony....5
(Notary Public Law: Section 5)

An applicant for notary public shall not have been convicted of or pled guilty or "nolo contendere" to a **felony** or a lesser offense incompatible with the duties of a notary public during the **5**-year period preceding the date of the application.

A. 2
(Notary Public Law: Section 6)

Application for Reappointment. to the office of notary public shall be filed at least **two** months prior to the expiration of the commission under which the notary is acting

---

MULTIPLE CHOICE QUESTIONS

If the notary changes his office address within the Commonwealth, notice in writing or electronically shall be given to the Secretary and the recorder of deeds of the county of original appointment by the notary within ___ days of such change.

A. 5
B. 10
C. 20
D. 30

Every notary, upon appointment and prior to entering the duties of notary public, shall take and subscribe the constitutional oath of office, and shall give a surety bond, payable to the Commonwealth of Pennsylvania, in the amount of $_____.

A. $ 5,000
B. $ 10,000
C. $ 15,000
D. $ 20,000

The notary public bond, as well as the commission and oath of office, shall be recorded in the _____ of the county in which the notary maintains an office at the time of appointment or reappointment.
A. office of the chief clerk
B. comptroller's office
C. office of the recorder of deeds
D. fiduciary office

ANSWERS

A. 5
(Notary Public Law: Section 7)

If the notary changes his office address within the Commonwealth, notice in writing or electronically shall be given to the Secretary and the recorder of deeds of the county of original appointment by the notary within **5** days of such change.

B. $ 10,000
(Notary Public Law: Section 8)

Every notary, upon appointment and prior to entering the duties of notary public, shall take and subscribe the constitutional oath of office, and shall give a surety bond, payable to the Commonwealth of Pennsylvania, in the amount of **ten thousand dollars ($ 10,000)**.

C. office of the recorder of deeds
(Notary Public Law: Section 8)

The notary public bond, as well as the commission and oath of office, shall be recorded in the **office of the recorder of deeds** of the county in which the notary maintains an office at the time of appointment or reappointment.

MULTIPLE CHOICE QUESTIONS

If a notary public fails to give bond and cause the bond and the commission and oath to be recorded within ___ days after the beginning of the term, his commission shall be null and void.

A. 10
B. 15
C. 30
D. 45

The official notary signature shall be registered, in the "Notary Register" in the prothonotary's office of county where the notary maintains an office, within ____ days after appointment or reappointment.

A. 10
B. 15
C. 30
D. 45

If a notary moves his office to another county, he must within ____ days thereafter register his signature in the prothonotary's office of county where the notary maintains an office.

A. 10
B. 15
C. 20
D. 30

ANSWERS

D. 45
(Notary Public Law: Section 8)

If a notary public fails to give bond and cause the bond and the commission and oath to be recorded within **45** days after the beginning of the term, his commission shall be null and void.

D. 45
(Notary Public Law: Section 9)

The official notary signature shall be registered, in the "Notary Register" in the prothonotary's office of county where the notary maintains an office, within **45** days after appointment or reappointment. (In counties of the second class, such signature shall also be registered in the clerk of courts' office within said period.)

D. 30
(Notary Public Law: Section)

If a notary moves his office to another county, he must within **30** days thereafter register his signature in the prothonotary's office of county where the notary maintains an office. (In counties of the second class, such signature shall also be registered in the clerk of courts' office within said period.)

MULTIPLE CHOICE QUESTIONS

In acting as a notary public, a notary shall sign the notary's name exactly and only as it appears on the _____ or otherwise execute the notary's electronic signature in a manner that attributes such signature to the notary public identified on the commission.

A. birth certificate
B. social security card
C. notary public commission
D. graduation certificate

Whenever the name of any notary is changed by decree of court, or otherwise, such notary may continue to perform official acts, in the name in which he was commissioned, until _____.

A. the expiration of 10 days.
B. the expiration of 30 days.
C. the end of the calendar year.
D. the expiration of his term.

RULONA is the abbreviation for _____.

A. Redrafted Unaltered Law on Notarial Acts
B. Reviewed Unmodified Law on Notarial Acts
C. Reworked Uniform Law on Notarial Acts
D. Revised Uniform Law on Notarial Acts

ANSWERS

C. notary public commission
(Notary Public Law: Section 9)

In acting as a notary public, a notary shall sign the notary's name exactly and only as it appears on the **commission** or otherwise execute the notary's electronic signature in a manner that attributes such signature to the notary public identified on the commission.

D. the expiration of his term.
(Notary Public Law: Section 10)

Whenever the name of any notary is changed by decree of court, or otherwise, such notary may continue to perform official acts, in the name in which he was commissioned, until the **expiration of his term.**

D. Revised Uniform Law on Notarial Acts
(RULONA 301)

RULONA is the abbreviation for **Revised Uniform Law on Notarial Acts**.

MULTIPLE CHOICE QUESTIONS

"_____" is a declaration in front of a notary that:
(1) the person signed the record for the reason stated in the record; and that
(2) if the person signed as a representative, he did so with proper authority.

A. transfiguration
B. bonafied statement
C. acknowledgment
D. assessment

"_____" is a declaration made by an individual on oath or affirmation before a notarial officer, that a statement in a record is true. The term includes an affidavit.

A. statement
B. Verification on oath or affirmation
C. soliloquy
D. affirment

If a notary public performs a notarial act in which he has a pecuniary interest in the transaction, the notarial act is

_____.

A. financially sound
B. monetarily recorded
C. permissible
D. voidable

ANSWERS

C. acknowledgment
(RULONA 302)

"Acknowledgment" is a declaration in front of a notary that:
(1) the person signed the record for the reason stated in the record; and that
(2) if the person signed as a representative, he did so with proper authority.

B. Verification on oath or affirmation
(RULONA 302)

"Verification on oath or affirmation" is a declaration, made by an individual on oath or affirmation before a notarial officer, that a statement in a record is true. The term includes an affidavit.

D. voidable
(RULONA 304)

If a notary public performs a notarial act in which he has a pecuniary interest in the transaction, the notarial act is **voidable**.

MULTIPLE CHOICE QUESTIONS

If a notarial act relates to a statement made in or a signature executed on a record, person making statement or executing signature shall appear _____ before the notary.

A. by telephone
B. text message
C. by video conference
D. personally

A notarial act shall be evidenced by a _____.

A. copy of the document.
B. transcript of judgment.
C. certificate.
D. certified copy of the ID.

A notarial certificate must be executed:

A. 24 hours before the acknowledgment.
B. contemporaneously with the performance of the notarial act.
C. in front of 2 witnesses.
D. with malintent.

ANSWERS

D. personally
(RULONA 306)

If a notarial act relates to a statement made in or a signature executed on a record, person making statement or executing signature shall appear **personally** before the notary.

C. certificate
(RULONA 315)

A notarial act shall be evidenced by a **certificate**.

B. contemporaneously with the performance of the notarial act.
(RULONA 315)

A notarial certificate must be executed **contemporaneously with the performance of the notarial act.**

MULTIPLE CHOICE QUESTIONS

A notarial certificate must identify the county and _____ in which the notarial act is performed.

A. town
B. village
C. city
D. state

The certificate of a notary must indicate the date of _____ of the notarial officer's commission.

A. commencement
B. anniversary
C. expiration
D. initiation

Who is responsible for the security of the stamping device of the notary public?

A. the county clerk
B. the register of deeds
C. the Secretary of the Commonwealth
D. the notary public

ANSWERS

D. state
(RULONA 315)

A notarial certificate must identify the county and **State** in which the notarial act is performed.

C. expiration
(RULONA 315)

The certificate of a notary must indicate the date of **expiration** of the notarial officer's commission.

D. the notary public
(RULONA 318)

The **notary public** is responsible for the security of the stamping device of the notary public.

MULTIPLE CHOICE QUESTIONS

A notary public shall maintain a journal in which the notary public records in _____ order all notarial acts that the notary public performs.

A. lunar calendar
B. chronological
C. alphabetical
D. limit

If the journal is maintained on a tangible medium, it shall be a bound register with _____ pages.

A. 8.5 X 11 inches
B. numbered
C. more than 100
D. white

On death or incompetency of a notary public, the personal representative or guardian shall deliver the notary journal within ___ days to the office of recorder of deeds in county where notary maintained his office.

A. 30
B. 45
C. 60
D. 15

ANSWERS

B. chronological
(RULONA 319)

A notary public shall maintain a journal in which the notary public records in **chronological** order all notarial acts that the notary public performs.

B. numbered
(RULONA 319)

If the journal is maintained on a tangible medium, it shall be a bound register with **numbered** pages.

A. 30
(RULONA 319)

On death or incompetency of a notary public, the personal representative or guardian shall deliver the notary journal within **30** days to the office of recorder of deeds in county where notary maintained his office.

MULTIPLE CHOICE QUESTIONS

Before a notary performs the initial notarial act with respect to an electronic record, a notary public shall notify the _____ that the notary will be performing notarial acts with respect to electronic records and identify each technology the notary intends to use.
A. county clerk
B. chief clerk
C. county assessor
D. department

An applicant for appointment and commission as a notary public must be able to read and write _____.

A. Spanish and English
B. at least English and one other language
C. three languages
D. English

An applicant for appointment and commission as a notary public must be at least ____ years of age and be a citizen or _____ of the United States.

A. 21...foreign national
B. 18...permanent legal resident
C. 21...alien resident
D. 18...temporary resident

ANSWERS

D. department
(RULONA 320)

Before a notary performs the initial notarial act with respect to an electronic record, a notary public shall notify the **department** that the notary will be performing notarial acts with respect to electronic records and identify each technology the notary intends to use.

D. English
(RULONA 321)

An applicant for appointment and commission as a notary public must be able to read and write <u>English</u>.

B. 18...permanent resident
(RULONA 321)

An applicant for appointment and commission as a notary public must be at least **18** years of age and be a citizen or **permanent legal resident** of the United States.

MULTIPLE CHOICE QUESTIONS

An applicant for appointment and commission as a notary public must be a resident or have a place of employment in _____ and be able to read and write _____.

A. this Commonwealth...English
B. Pennsylvania...two languages
C. this Commonwealth...Spanish
D. the county of appointment...two languages

A notary public application must be accompanied by a nonrefundable fee of $_____, payable to the Commonwealth of Pennsylvania. This amount shall include the application fee for notary public commission and fee for filing of the bond with the department.
A. $ 30
B. $ 42
C. $ 50
D. $ 65

The surety or issuing entity must give ___ days' notice to the department before canceling the notary bond.

A. 10
B. 15
C. 20
D. 30

ANSWERS

A. this Commonwealth...English
(RULONA 321)

An applicant for appointment and commission as a notary public must be a resident or have a place of employment in **this Commonwealth** and be able to read and write **English**.

B. $ 42
(RULONA 321)

A notary public application must be accompanied by a nonrefundable fee of **$42**, payable to the Commonwealth of Pennsylvania. This amount shall include the application fee for notary public commission and fee for filing of the bond with the department.

D. 30
(RULONA 321)

The surety or issuing entity must give **30** days' notice to the department before canceling the notary bond. Also, the surety or issuing entity shall notify the department not later than 30 days after making a payment to a claimant under the bond.

MULTIPLE CHOICE QUESTIONS

The official signature of each notary public shall be registered, for a fee of 50¢, in the "Notary Register" provided for that purpose in the _____of the county where the notary public maintains an office.

A. fiscal office
B. monetary records
C. fees and registration
D. prothonotary's office

The official signature of each notary public shall be registered within: (i) ____ days after appointment or reappointment; and (ii) ____ days after moving to a different county.

A. 30...45
B. 30...60
C. 45...30
D. 45...60

Within ____ days of recording the bond, oath of office and commission in the office of the recorder of deeds, a copy of the bond and oath of office must be filed with the department.

A. 30
B. 60
C. 90
D. 15

ANSWERS

D. prothonotary's office
(RULONA 321)

The official signature of each notary public shall be registered, for a fee of 50¢, in the "Notary Register" provided for that purpose in the **prothonotary's** office of the county where the notary public maintains an office.

C. 45...30
(RULONA 321)

The official signature of each notary public shall be registered within: (i) **45** days after appointment or reappointment; and (ii) **30** days after moving to a different county.

C. 90
(RULONA 321)

Within **90** days of recording the bond, oath of office and commission in the office of the recorder of deeds, a copy of the bond and oath of office must be filed with the department.

MULTIPLE CHOICE QUESTIONS

The department may impose an administrative penalty of up to $_____ on a notary public for each act or omission which constitutes a violation of RULONA.

A. $ 250
B. $ 500
C. $ 750
D. $ 1,000

A notary public who is not an attorney may not use the terms_____ or _____.

A. notary public or notary
B. "notario" or "notario publico"
C. notary or notary public
D. none of the above

The department may require applicants for appointment and commission as notaries public to submit _____ history record information as provided in 18 Pa.C.S. Ch. 91.
A. criminal
B. tax
C. school
D. bank

ANSWERS

D. $ 1,000
(RULONA 323)

The department may impose an administrative penalty of up to **$1,000** on a notary public for each act or omission which constitutes a violation of RULONA. (May also be imposed on any person who performs a notarial act without being properly appointed and commissioned.)

B. "notario" or "notario publico"
(RULONA 325)

A notary public who is not an attorney **may not** use the term "notario" or "notario publico".

A. criminal
(RULONA 327)

The department may require applicants for appointment and commission as notaries public to submit **criminal** history record information as provided in 18 Pa.C.S. Ch. 91.

MULTIPLE CHOICE QUESTIONS

www.dos.pa.gov

The fee for taking an acknowledgment is _____.:

A. $ 2
B. $ 3
C. $ 4
D. $ 5

---

www.dos.pa.gov

The fee for taking an acknowledgment (each additional name) is _____.

A. $ 2
B. $ 3
C. $ 4
D. $ 5

---

www.dos.pa.gov

The fee for administering oath or affirmation (per individual taking oath or affirmation) is _____.

A. $ 2
B. $ 3
C. $ 4
D. $ 5

ANSWERS

D. 5
(www.dos.pa.gov)

The fee for taking an acknowledgment is **$ 5.**

A. $ 2
(www.dos.pa.gov)

The fee for taking an acknowledgment (each additional name) is **$ 2**

D. $ 5
(www.dos.pa.gov)

The fee for administering oath or affirmation (per individual taking oath or affirmation) is **$ 5**.

MULTIPLE CHOICE QUESTIONS

www.dos.pa.gov

The fee for taking verification on oath or affirmation (no matter how many signatures) is _____.

A. $ 2
B. $ 3
C. $ 4
D. $ 5

www.dos.pa.gov

The fee for witnessing or attesting a signature (per signature) is _____.

A. $ 2
B. $ 3
C. $ 4
D. $ 5

www.dos.pa.gov

The fee for certifying or attesting a copy or deposition (per certified copy) is _____.

A. $ 2
B. $ 3
C. $ 4
D. $ 5

ANSWERS

D. $ 5
(www.dos.pa.gov)

The fee for taking verification on oath or affirmation (no matter how many signatures) is **$ 5**.

D. $ 5
(www.dos.pa.gov)

The fee for witnessing or attesting a signature (per signature) is **$ 5**.

D. $ 5
(www.dos.pa.gov)

The fee for certifying or attesting a copy or deposition (per certified copy) is **$ 5**.

MULTIPLE CHOICE QUESTIONS

---

www.dos.pa.gov

The fee for noting a protest of a negotiable instrument (per page) is _____.

A. $ 2
B. $ 3
C. $ 4
D. $ 5

---

www.dos.pa.gov

Notaries may charge fees as set by _____.

A. the county clerk
B. the register of deeds
C. the Pennsylvania State Comptroller
D. the Department of State

---

www.dos.pa.gov

Fees may be _____ by notaries

A. doubled
B. waived
C. increased
D. tripled

ANSWERS

B. $ 3
(www.dos.pa.gov)

The fee for noting a protest of a negotiable instrument (per page) is **$ 3**.

D. the Department of State
(www.dos.pa.gov)

Notaries may charge fees as set by the **Department of State**.

B. waived
(www.dos.pa.gov)

Fees may be **waived** by notaries.

MULTIPLE CHOICE QUESTIONS

Which of the following does not appear on the official stamp of a notary public?
A. The words "Commonwealth of Pennsylvania – Notary Seal."
B. The date of birth of the notary public.
C. The name as it appears on the commission of the notary and the words "Notary Public."
D. The name of the county in which the notary public maintains an office.

Which of the following does not appear on the official stamp of a notary public?
A. The date the notary's current commission expires.
B. The seven-digit commission identification number assigned by the Department.
C. The words "Notary Public."
D. The date the notary's current commission commenced.

Which of the following statements is not correct?
A. No words or terms on the official stamp may be abbreviated.
B. The official stamp or notary seal shall be stamped or affixed to the notarial certificate near the notary's signature or attached to or logically associated with an electronic record containing the notary's signature.
C. A notary public may place an imprint of the notary's official stamp over any signature in a record to be notarized or over any writing in a notarial certificate.
D. A notary public shall not alter or deface the official stamp.

ANSWERS

B. The date of birth of the notary public.
(RULONA Regulations 167.21)

D. The date the notary's current commission commenced.
(RULONA Regulations 167.21)

C. is not correct.
(RULONA Regulations 167.21)

A notary public shall NOT place an imprint of the notary's official stamp over any signature in a record to be notarized or over any writing in a notarial certificate.

MULTIPLE CHOICE QUESTIONS

Which of the following statements is not correct?
A. Notary public may use an embossed or crimped image in the performance of a notarial act.
B. Use of embosser can be only in conjunction with the use of an official stamp.
C. Embosser cannot be placed over signature or printed material.
D. Notary public may use any other notary public's embosser or any other object in lieu of the notary public's official stamp to perform a notarial act.

Which of the following is not correct? A notary journal must contain:
A. The name of the notary public as it appears on his birth
   certificate.
B. The notary public's commission number;
C. The notary public's commission expiration date;
D. The notary public's office address of record with the Department;

Which of the following is not correct? A notary journal must contain:

A. Statement that in the event of death of the notary public, journal shall be delivered or mailed to the office of the recorder of deeds in the country where the notary last maintained an office;
B. The meaning of any not commonly abbreviated word or symbol used in recording a notarial act in the notarial journal;
C. The signature of the notary public;
D. A copy of the will of the notary public.

ANSWERS

D is not correct. It should read:

Notary public **shall not** use any other notary public's embosser or any other object in lieu of the notary public's official stamp to perform a notarial act.
(RULONA Regulations 167.23)

A is not correct. It should read:

A. The name of the notary public as it appears **on the commission.**
(RULONA Regulations 167.31)

D. A copy of the will of the notary public.
(RULONA Regulations 167.31)

This is not a requirement.

MULTIPLE CHOICE QUESTIONS

Which of the following is not correct? Prohibited entries in a notary public journal include an individual's first name or first initial and last name in combination with and linked to any one or more of the following data elements when the data elements are not encrypted or redacted:
A. Social Security number.
B. Driver's license number
C. Financial account number, credit or debit card number, with any required security code or access code
D. The fee paid by the receiver of the notarial service.

Which of the following is not correct?
Records for which a notary may not issue a certified copy include:
A. Vital Records (birth and death certificates)
B. U.S. Naturalization Certificates
C. Any government-issued record which on its face states "do not copy," or "illegal to copy" etc.
D Any record which is allowed by law to copy or certify

Which of the following is correct?
Records for which a notary may not issue a certified copy include:
A. Private records, leases
B. Drivers' licenses, Transcripts, Bills of sale
C. Diplomas, Contracts, medical records
D. U.S. Naturalization Certificates

ANSWERS

D. The fee paid by the receiver of the notarial service.
(RULONA Regulations 167.32)

D is not correct because it is not one of the items listed in this section and is a required notation.

D is not correct

This should read:
D. Any record which is **prohibited** by law to copy or certify.
(RULONA Regulations 167.65)

D. U.S. Naturalization Certificates

Notaries may **NOT** issue a certified copy of a U.S. Naturalization Certificate. Therefore, the answer is D.
(RULONA Regulations 167.65)

Made in the USA
Coppell, TX
24 August 2021

61107768R00070